Laughter yoga for joy

Laughter yoga for joy is an awareness & movement-based approach to laughter yoga.

This book is a journey into this process which deepens your experience of joy in day-to-day life.

You will be shown how to use all your resources - your body, breath, emotions & feelings, mind, spirit and awareness - to reclaim and expand the joy in your life.

Reviews include: *'I love this book so much - it's so practical, with really clear writing, and an encouraging feel throughout. I really like laughter yoga but I especially like Joe's form of it, which is less focused on doing*

D1607884

"exercises" and more focused on spontaneous playfulness....The practice described inside could be beneficial to anyone.... a very good practice for dealing with LIFE!'

(Philip Cowell, Good Chance Theatre)

'Joe.... with the help of other voices in the laughter yoga movement, extends an invitation "to experience the joy of being alive." The process is not prescriptive. But instead, an infinitely creative, movement-based way to create increased presence, and develop an ever-expansive joy as a way of being.'

(Mary Ann Duffy, Laughter Yoga Leader and Artist)

Laughter yoga for joy

Preface

This book starts with a thank you.

Over the decades, many thousands of you have helped shape this book, many of you not even members of the laughter yoga family. Consciously or not there have been contributions worldwide from different cultures, different businesses, and different ways of life. I hear the voices and see the faces of so many behind-the-scenes influences.

Over the years, thousands from the laughter tribe and the laughter yoga family have contributed. Again, I see so many faces and hear so many voices. I thank you all.

I give a thank you to the specific contributors from each chapter. In chronological order this is Dr Madan Kataria, Duncan Cook, Eser Mutlu, Fabrice Loizeau, Marie Christine, Lee Jean, Kitty Haha, and Shifra Arwas.

There are two other major contributions.

The first is my JOYBeats colleagues, Keyem and Shifra. It has been almost indescribably wonderful to create our events together.

The second is Karima and her 'Togetherness Group' which started at the beginning of the global pandemic, and which provided weekly opportunities for growth and exploration.

I thank you all from the bottom of my heart.

Introduction part 1

Dear reader,

I invite you to join me on a journey into laughter yoga for joy.

I invite you to deepen your experience of this process as you journey into joy.

Fortunately, there is no wrong way of doing it. Your own way is the right way, and you will progress at the right speed because it is not a race.

This process is best done gently and with your full awareness. Like a flower unfurling, you will develop in your own unique and perfect way.

You will probably find that as you focus on your awareness, it expands. If so, you will find there is always more to be aware of. Therefore, you find that with increased awareness even simple exercises and practices become more engaging and more profound. They become more connecting and have greater impact. This happens because as you practise being aware, you begin to realise you can be aware of your own awareness.

All stillness practices help. Zazen or watching the breath is a classic stillness practice and helps us be grounded and aware of our awareness.

This is a major inner development because once you become aware of your own awareness, your experience of time changes beyond description. Not only do you become aware of present-moment awareness or the 'NOW', but you begin to experience its vastness and its potential.

Your 'NOW' can be a bigger experience than ever before.

This process leads us to the heart of laughter yoga for joy.

Do you remember the saying '*What we focus on, expands*'? Not only is joy in the 'now' but when we focus on the joy in the now, it expands. So, the process in laughter yoga for joy is to connect with and expand your joy in the 'NOW'.

This takes practice but it is an expansive and connecting experience with infinite potential.

Shall we begin?

'The way is simple, but the crooked path is more popular.'

Lao Tsu

Introduction part 2

'I like the energy Joe brings to laughter yoga. I like his embodied movement-based approach and the way this helps people experience joy in their laughter yoga'

Dr Madan Kataria, Founder of the Global Laughter Yoga Movement.

Laughter yoga for joy is awareness & movement-based laughter yoga. It is a process not a prescription and helps us live in the moment joyfully.

It starts as a personal practice which we blend effortlessly into our own sessions, with three main aims.

- This first is to energise us so that we feel alive.

- The second is to keep us relaxing into the moment.
- The third is to help us find calm, peace, and clarity.

It is a whole being approach to laughter yoga.

In this approach we use all our resources, our body, breath, feelings & emotions, mind, spirit, environment, and awareness. In our sessions we also use the presence, energy, and inspiration of our fellow humans in ways described below.

It is an in-the-moment approach. In our own practice as well as in our sessions it is naturally spontaneous and creative where anything and everything can become a new exercise. It flows. As a result, the experience becomes more engaging.

This in-the-moment quality helps us feel more connected and therefore more alive.

The process is free-flowing and non-prescriptive but subtly and carefully structured with a beginning, middle and end. This makes it both spontaneous and focused and so helps it maintain its energy and have an effortless rhythm. As a result, laughter is natural, relaxed, hearty, and unconditional.

In this approach there are sometimes no formal exercises. Exercises are magnificent and fun but are not essential. They have a supportive and often unplanned role which makes them free flowing, effortless, and unique. They are usually inspired by observations and interactions from fellow participants, when someone says or does something that catches your attention. This makes the exercises creative and spontaneous and therefore funnier, more engaging – and more joyful. In this process the group recognises that it has an active role and that it owns the experience. This gives your laughter yoga the biggest possible impact.

Let's explore the process itself.

'Believe nothing, no matter where you read it or who has said it, not even if I have said it, unless it agrees with your own reason and your own common sense'

Buddha.

Introduction part 3

'I consider this valuable Continuing Professional Development for laughter yoga practitioners'

Duncan Cook, Laughter Yoga Master Trainer in Canada

The laughter yoga for joy process treats laughter as prana or chi. You raise energy and then embody and ground it, both in your own practice and in your sessions.

First, we practise increasing and expanding it through movement-based exercises. Next, we embody it, so we feel it in our body and in our being. Finally, we ground it through breathing and meditation practices. The movement, embodiment and breathing are as simple as possible so that our attention and awareness remain focused in the experience.

Awareness and stillness are the keys.

This process means we side-step our egoic and analytical mind and connect with our being - our inner awareness and soul. Sometimes we experience cathartic release as memories, past hurts and painful experiences have their sting washed away, without specific attention being drawn to them. This is a gentle, wholesome, and cleansing process which calms the monkey mind and leads us into stillness and inner peace.

Stillness and awareness of peace and calm are at the heart of laughter yoga for joy.

All stillness invites us to be aware of our own experience. The stillness we experience after the simple, whole-being, movement-based approach is often surprisingly profound.

This stillness deepens as we practice noticing our awareness.

When we emerge from this profound stillness, we almost always experience insights. When we receive them with open-hearted, non-critical listening we experience additional clarity and transformation.

The simplicity of the process can be challenging but it feeds our inner awareness and helps us grow and be at our best. This deepens our connection to joy.

We can all learn this approach so let's explore this process in more detail.

'Learning is not compulsory... neither is survival.'

W. Edwards Deming

Chapter 1

Move into joy.

'Finding inner joy starting with your own body movement.'

Eser Mutlu, Laughter Yoga Master Trainer in Turkey.

'I met Joe Hoare 2018 when he came to the Laughter Yoga Istanbul Conference. He had a workshop in our Conference...... This was something different and still we were laughing....... Different but effective.

Then we met again in the Paris Conference 2019. He also had a workshop in Paris and when I participated, I laughed and cried at the end. This was perfect releasing of emotions... And I remember I felt happy that I am alive ... This was totally different feeling.

This year I asked him to teach this to my leaders those days I was giving online leader training.

Yes, for me perfect way of finding Joy, our spirit, and releasing emotions.

Thank you, Joe, for showing another way of finding Joy and thank you for being my friend.'

Move. Just move your body.

Laughter yoga for joy starts with movement. Movement immediately starts to take our attention out of our head. Your movement can be free and spontaneous, and it can also be structured. Both these approaches work – just move your body.

It doesn't matter which part of your body you start moving, nor whether you're seated, lying, or standing. Movements can be big or small, either fast or slow, either vigorous or lethargic. The key is to bring the whole body into movement, gradually and progressively until you feel movement in every body part.

The next step is to keep the body moving. We often tend to move our body and then stop and return to being stationary again. In laughter yoga for joy, we develop the practice of continuous, whole-body movement so that our body remembers what it feels like to move and, importantly, to keep experiencing being in movement. The more we practise this, the more we are building our own muscle memory and forming a connection in our own consciousness between movement and getting out of our head.

The practice of continuous movement becomes our anchor. It is the point to which we always return, especially when we notice attention has returned to our thoughts and our head, or we have stopped moving.

When we use our body to get out of our head, we experience the present moment. Joy only exists in the present moment, so movement becomes our anchor for joy.

This usually requires endless and repeated practice, but it becomes increasingly joyful.

Although it doesn't matter what part of the body we move first, it often works well to start either with the shoulders or the hands & wrists. As a personal practice it is often good to start with hands & wrists because this can be personally engaging. It can be fun to examine our own fingers and hands in creative and spontaneous movement, which means we will start to relax and smile.

As a group practice it is often good to start with shoulders because shoulder shrugging is visually engaging and rapidly leads to group connection and natural spontaneous genuine laughter.

It is helpful to remember that the best movements to start with depend on the circumstances at the time. It is good to have a flexible approach and, when appropriate, be prepared to start movements by standing up or maybe using our feet. When we use our whole body as a resource, we become free to start our movement and embodied awareness with any body part we choose.

Once we have started moving, we gradually involve our whole body. It is good to remember that our head and face are part of our body and specifically involve them as well. As we know, smiling and laughing relax our face so when we include them as well, we have successfully engaged our whole body.

Whole body movement always generates genuine, spontaneous, good-hearted smiling and laughter. With practice, this becomes sustained and unconditional because it is an expression of the joy of being alive.

Whole body movement with present-moment awareness become a doorway to our inner joy.

Let's explore this further.

'Hard times require furious dancing'

African saying.

'Common sense and a sense of humour are the same thing, moving at different speeds. A sense of humour is just common sense, dancing.'

William James

Chapter 2

Do not be afraid to be yourself.

'Joe is a UFO in laughter yoga.'

Fabrice Loizeau, Laughter Yoga Master Trainer in France.

'I was lucky to meet him at a laughter yoga conference in Turkey with Madan Kataria and his performance was both original and very captivating. All the participants really enjoyed his workshop.

The following year, I appointed him as a speaker at the International Laughter Yoga Congress that I organized with Dr Kataria: France (and the 28 other nations) were thus able to discover Joe's Laughter Yoga.... He knows how to engage his audience; his actions are refreshing ...... Since then, he is my guest on the French online Laughter yoga sessions.'

Laughter yoga for joy encourages you to be your beautiful self. There is no wrong way of doing it, there is simply your way. Remember that you are unique - just like everyone else - so focus on being you.

The more you focus on being yourself in laughter yoga, the more original, creative, and authentic you become. The more authentic you are, the more you encourage everyone else to be authentic too. Authenticity is a life-enhancing quality even when the particular experience is not to your own taste.

In laughter yoga for joy, authentic movement means both being in movement and being aware of the present moment. It is presence in movement. It is a form of moving yoga nidra. Although everyone moves in their own way, when you combine this with present-moment awareness you develop your ability to communicate through your own unique style – in Fabrice's words, you become a UFO.

When you express the present moment through movement, you realise that because every moment is unique, so too is the movement that expresses it. This is a liberating approach because it means you can move spontaneously and creatively and intuitively, as is appropriate at the time. You do not need to follow or learn a prescribed sequence because the right movement will be new and fresh each time.

In a session and in your own practice, sometimes you might start by moving your shoulders, sometimes by moving your head and neck, sometimes by smiling and facial yoga, sometimes by moving your hands or feet. You are free to move as is appropriate in the moment and to be guided by it. The more you practise being by the moment through being aware of it and expressing it through movement, the more creative and flowing your style becomes.

It also becomes more authentic and enjoyable.

You need to practise random movement. If you are familiar with the dance style known as 5 Rhythms, this is called 'chaos'. The more you practise moving your body in unplanned and irregular and spontaneous ways, the more liberating, expressive, and unique your body communication becomes.

When you add laughter yoga awareness to this process, it becomes increasingly joyful. The easiest way to add this awareness is to relax your face and to smile while moving. With practice you can feel your inner smile and allow your movements to express this. In the same way that your smile is naturally warm and engaging, this makes your movements warm and engaging too.

The more you practise connecting with your inner smile, the more you strengthen your connection with joy and the more your smile becomes an expression of joy. In this way when your movement becomes an expression of your inner smile it is also an expression of joy.

When your movements become an expression of joy, they are also an expression of your unique and beautiful self.

How does this make you feel?

'Follow your bliss'

Joseph Campbell

Chapter 3

Embrace the moment.

'To feel alive ….. the best feeling of all!'

Marie-Christine, Laughter Ambassador from Austria.

"Are you feeling alive?"

Joe is a joy giver. In his sessions he comes directly to the essence of LY: unconditional laughter and unconditional love. He unites many different nationalities and makes the participants embrace every moment and to enjoy the little things in life.

How? Not by performing "classical" LY exercises, but repetition of positive affirmations and by adding laughter to daily activities or simply while pointing at various objects in the room. We don't have time to think, we follow his lead and laugh along!

Indeed, breathing and laughing with Joe makes me feel alive. ...the best feeling of all!'

Laughter yoga for joy helps you feel alive – *'the best feeling of all'* as Marie Christine describes. As mentioned in the introduction, feeling alive is its first purpose. The more attention you bring to the present moment, the more alive you feel. The more you smile at the same time, the more enjoyable the experience of being alive.

A question for everyone is how alive can you feel?

As you have seen already, movement helps you connect with the present moment. In laughter yoga for joy, the more you focus on free and spontaneous movement, the faster you arrive in the present moment. The more you are aware of the present moment, the more you experience being alive. The more you smile, especially inside, the more you can experience the joy of being alive.

'We don't have time to think', Marie Christine said. Thinking, analysing, comparing, and criticising interrupt your connection to the present moment. Movement is an immediate and effective antidote to this. With practice, movement can bring you into the present moment instantly. The more you're in the moment, the more alive you can feel.

Breath is the other traditional and proven route to help you connect with the present moment. 'Breath' starts with awareness of your breath, the simple act of noticing that you are breathing. This fundamental step applies in laughter yoga for joy where you combine the breath awareness with your movements. You start by gradually becoming aware of your breathing at the same time as you are moving. You do this without allowing your new awareness to interrupt the flow of your movements. It is often helpful to start by moving slowly rather than vigorously so that it is easy to combine your breath and movements. You want this new expansion to be easy and effortless, but you want to keep moving as well. If your breath awareness disturbs your flow, make your movements simpler and slower until you find your own inner balance. It is there, waiting for you.

When you find this place, dive into it, embrace it, dance with it.

The next step is to relax and, importantly, to keep relaxing into this place of effortless inner balance. When you keep your movements and your breathing relaxed, simple, and effortless, you can focus your attention on your awareness. This process side steps the monkey mind and allows your experience of the present moment to expand and help you feel calm, peaceful, and joyful.

This can be a cathartic experience. People often experience an inner healing because the process of being present often allows the sting of memories and past experiences to gently wash away. There is no focus other than being present with effortless movement, and breathing and relaxing into the moment, and sometimes this allows an inner transformation to happen.

The more we embrace this process, the more we allow our inner awareness to grow and expand. It becomes possible to move faster and more vigorously while still being grounded and connected to both body and breath. The more you practise this, the more you can explore saying connected and aware during different styles of movement. This is a profound practice because it is easy to become too absorbed in the movement that you forget the breath and your awareness. It helps to keep the practice as simple as possible and expand from this simplicity.

The more we expand, the more alive we feel – *'the best feeling of all'*.

'Out beyond ideas of

Wrongdoing and rightdoing

There is a field.

I'll meet you there.'

Rumi

'Do something wonderful, people may imitate it.'

Albert Schweitzer

Chapter 4

Go with the flow.

'Every session is unique.'

Lee Jean, Laughter Yoga Ambassador in Malaysia.

'I find Joe's approach in his zoom laughter enlightening….. pleasant, composed…. Every session is different, and Joe goes with the flow, making each session unique, like having a different theme for every session. His approach is acceptable by most cultures and applicable in international arena.

It's refreshing & I like his style of having different variation of laughter breathing techniques, encompassing playfulness which eventually enhances effectiveness wholesomely.

At times, music was incorporated where one can dance and sing along, feeling joy and playfulness. With his gentle, accommodating approach, I felt comfortable & energised at the end of his sessions.

You have to attend to find out why and to experience the Joy... Hohohahahahahahahahahaha'

'The influence of a vital person vitalises, there's no doubt about it ...... and the only way to do that is to find in your own case where the life is and become alive yourself.'

Joseph Campbell

In the previous chapters you've read how a process of movement, breath, and awareness helps you come alive.

When you use these insights and principles to develop your own practice, you experience an expansion and an experience of feeling more and more alive. This feeling is unique to everyone and the more you trust it, the more you will go with your own flow. This flow is unique because it emerges from your own being. It is your own self-generated sunshine. It is a natural beacon and people feel it, especially in your sessions.

Flow and the experience of being alive are timeless because they are 'NOW'. Therefore, they both allow and invite you to be spontaneous. They also allow you to be generous and inclusive because when you understand flow you realise it incorporates all movement, breath, and awareness. Life flows like a river and so does laughter yoga for joy.

When you integrate your movement and breath with your joyful awareness, you become centred in your uniqueness and authenticity and your experience of being alive. At the same time, you are also connected with your circumstances, for example the group you're with, and feeling the ebb and flow of their energy. In this way you connect with laughter chi, the joyful vital energy of life. When you flow in this way, every session is unique because like the river in flow, you are never in the same place again and you are constantly responding to the now.

Laughter yoga for joy invites you to keep flowing and connecting joyfully with the now.

This flow is liberating and practical. For example, whether you decide to use music or props or exercises, you are always flowing with laughter chi. Your laughter chi is not dependant on them but supports you as necessary. This allows you to be infinitely flexible and spontaneous.

The flow of laughter chi is naturally playful and holistic and energising. It has a light and engaging quality. It is non-judgemental and has the potential to blend differences into harmony. It is gently accommodating.

Laughter chi is also empowering because it does not force or compel but invites. The more you learn to flow with your it, the easier it becomes to incorporate ideas and suggestions that your participants introduce. Laughter chi is therefore empowering for everyone as it maximises everyone's engagement. Everyone becomes an active co-creator in the evolving flow and because this flow invites engagement rather than forces it, it allows everyone to find their own level. As Lee Jean observed, this is a comfortable, energising and life enhancing experience, so find your flow.

The steps so far include:

- whole body movement where you relax into your own movement

- awareness of your breathing at the same time as being in movement
- relaxing into your inner peace, calm, and balance.

The progression is to practise being aware of this. as you do, you will start to feel a deeper connection with stillness and therefore joy.

'Find the place inside you where there's joy, and the joy will burn out the pain'.

Joseph Campbell

'The greatest discovery of my generation is that a person can alter their life simply by altering their attitude of mind.'

William James

Chapter 5

Trust

'Be your true self, free of inhibitions.'

Kitty Haha, Laughter Yoga Master Trainer in Hong Kong.

'Yet he knows how to help everyone tune in the group dynamics, feeling safe and comfortable, relaxing, and genuine, and together co-create joy and enjoy the magic bond through laughter that is unique to all present in the moment.

Joe is the captain, and we all are in the same boat sailing along with the flow to joy and genuineness

Going with the flow, we enjoy all the ups and downs (just different emotions and feelings, no judgment here) Sometimes it's calm and peaceful, sometimes we are so crazy, wild with joy and excited, like rocking in the sea, or in a roller coaster.

The best thing about joining this journey with Joe is it's stress-free! In a second everyone can open up, be his/her true self, free of inhibitions and express all feelings freely, creatively, and honestly

There is a unique kind of 'trust' in this group, often comprising people who are complete strangers to each other. What changes this strange space into a secure atmosphere in an instant?

Laughter yoga for joy has a special kind of trust.

It starts in each of us individually and develops with experience. It is laughter yoga as a service, framed with a healing intention. This intention allows sessions to flow and to be guided by something that knows better than us.

This flow is inherently joyful and liberating and includes a recognition of our connection, our shared humanity. It is intuitive and connecting and it is felt by participants.

There are practical steps for developing this flow and this trust.

We start by knowing our material so well that we never do laughter yoga. Through attention, intention, and repetition (AIR if you like acronyms) we immerse ourselves in laughter yoga qualities and so reach a state where we breathe, move and live laughter yoga.

By comparison, when we do laughter yoga, there are times when we are not doing it. There is a separation between us and laughter yoga. We need to practise our laughter yoga until we stop 'doing' exercises and reach that place where it is as natural as breathing. In this way, exercises are no longer laughter yoga but life. The only way this happens is when we fully immerse ourselves in our laughter yoga and simply live it.

This does not mean every second is filled with laughter and joy, but it is our basic state which we are aware of and to which we always return.

Agatha Christie expressed it beautifully:

'I like living. I have sometimes been wildly, despairingly, acutely miserable, racked with sorrow, but through it all I still know quite certainly that just to be alive is a grand thing.'

When we use our laughter yoga to reconnect with this level of awareness we radiate a quality that people recognise intuitively. They feel they can trust it. This trust comes from our experience of trusting ourselves. To achieve this, we need to practise laughter yoga for joy especially when times are difficult. Usually in these circumstances the practice will include compassion and appreciation more than laughter. We might also choose to move our awareness away from our difficulties. Choice, compassion and appreciation are profound, liberating, and therefore life-enhancing experiences.

When we practise our laughter yoga for joy in this way it becomes our natural way of being. We feel more intensely than we used to because we are more aware and alive, and sometimes this is difficult. However, we are potentially more resilient because we are making better use of all our resources as the emotions pass.

A further step is to practise being guided. The healing dimension of laughter yoga for joy means we practise allowing inspiration to flow through us. It means trusting our intuition and trusting the flow and the laughter chi wherever it leads us. This requires considerable practice and experience but when we are

comfortable in this flow it evokes a
further level of trust.

Part of this process is being
grounded. 'Start with the end in
mind' is an excellent reminder from
Steven Covey's best-selling book '7
habits of highly effective people'. This
means we always know our
destination. Our destination needs to
include helping make the experience
relevant for all participants. We
achieve this through moments of
settling and stillness. These moments
offer us the opportunity to
recalibrate ourselves and find our
own level. They allow us to own our
experience.

Relaxation is a further benefit of this
level of practice. The more familiar
we become with this process, the
more we relax. The more we relax,

the more we implicitly invite everyone else to relax as well. This allows a deepening experience of relaxation.

There is no shortcut to this state. We need to practise diligently and continuously for a considerable time to reach this level of awareness and relaxation. The good news is that provided we keep practising regularly, it happens. The keys are constancy and consistency, using the variety of resources available to us including movement, breath and awareness. This means we can practise anywhere and at any time. We can practise invisibly where necessary. When we keep practising, we allow our inner space and our experience of stillness to keep expanding. This is a life-enhancing quality and people will feel it and tend to trust it.

These steps are what help create a *'secure atmosphere in an instant.'*

'Life is not complex. We are complex. Life is simple, and the simple thing is the right thing.'

Oscar Wilde

'Take time to laugh - it is the music of the soul.'

From an old English prayer.

Chapter 6

The Soul knows.

'Magic secret - Slowing down the pace of life and increasing body insight at the same time'

Shifra Arwas, Laughter Yoga Master Trainer in Israel.

''You bring with you calmness, seriousness, movement and vitality to the body, and then the soul understands the lesson it must go through.

*The insights slowly descend through the movement, the relaxed breathing, and the release of the sounds ....
and then we will discover how the laughter hurts from the stomach up. Illuminates us.*

The combination of silence, movement, breathing, and vocal release is Joe. It lets you be at your own pace, understanding of yourself and yourself slowly but vitally and yes .... we all need it in the madness of life around us. That's Joe's magic secret. Slowing down the pace of life and increasing body insight at the same time

Points about Joe:

You work with an inner silence.

We believe you...so, we trust you....so you transmit reliability.

You connect things from head to body and vice versa. You flow, letting us express ourselves.'

Laughter yoga for joy is a return to the soul.

It is an inner journey which uses all our resources, especially our embodiment. Our embodiment is our doorway through which we access all our physical senses. It is also the doorway to our awareness and our inner knowing.

Our body is key. When we connect with our body we get out of our head because movement and body awareness are an excellent antidote to the monkey mind. This antidote helps us 'get out of our own way'. It helps us replace overthinking with present-moment awareness. Present-moment awareness, a quiet mind, and stillness are the starting point for a conscious, aware, and joyful life. They are also the entry point for our soul because a quiet mind means we can hear the soul's messages.

Laughter yoga for joy helps us quiet our mind and hear our soul's messages.

'There is a voice that doesn't use words. Listen.'

Rumi

Laughter yoga for joy helps us find our optimum speed for moving through life. Many years ago, a conference speaker commented that there is an optimum speed for scanning a body with your hand. Too fast and you miss things. Too slowly and you get bogged in detail. In my experience, this principle applies to all body movement and laughter yoga for joy uses this insight of optimum speed.

We often move too fast. When we slow our body we allow it to harmonise with our soul. When we slow our body enough we become aware of the chi or life force flowing through it. When we become aware of this we can be in a magic place of simultaneously moving and listening. This is a place of intuition and effortlessness and one where we are potentially receptive to our soul's messages.

The process is to reconnect with our body awareness and to pay attention.

The shift that happens in laughter yoga for joy is that with focus, our attention gradually moves into our awareness. We energise this process by focusing initially on movement and our body in the simplest ways possible. We progressively move and relax and become aware of how this feels. We specifically include our face, head, and neck so that we become aware of our whole body. This process of connecting with our body and listening to its messages is itself a lifelong practice.

The next level is to become aware of our breathing while we are moving. We notice it, relax it, open our mouth, and relax our jaw and allow our outbreath to become audible, often by sighing. Again, we do this in the simplest possible way and therefore maintain a quality of effortlessness. This too is a lifelong practice.

The final ingredient is joy. As we relax our face in this process we are likely to start smiling naturally because the experience feels good. The more we smile the better we feel and therefore it is easy to produce a genuine, good-natured, joyful intentional laugh.

We have connected with our joy and this laugh comes from our soul.

This is a free and non-prescriptive process. There is no wrong way of doing it because we simply explore how we are. We come into the present moment, proceed at our own pace, release what needs releasing, express what needs expressing, and experience our own awareness.

This process often undermines the monkey mind without it being aware of being undermined. Sometimes the free movement and joy continue naturally, and we happen to notice them later. This is the effect of a simple and repeated practice which involves neither thinking nor learning. We are practising being alive.

When use all our resources we realise how much more there is to life than just thinking. This itself is a calming experience. We tend to find the monkey mind becomes quieter and this deepens our calm and our experience of stillness. When we are relaxed and calm and notice that we are relaxed and calm, we become calmer and even more relaxed. It is a positive and virtuous cycle.

The magic ingredient is then to colour this calm with joy. When we relax into the present moment and smile intentionally, we connect with the joy in our soul. This simple intentional act allows our soul to communicate with us.

Our soul knows. Let it speak. Listen.

'Joy is the cure to the sickness of the soul.'

Carlos Santana

'I have been confronted with many difficulties throughout the course of my life……. But I laugh often, and my laughter is contagious. When people ask me how I find the strength to laugh now, I reply that I am a professional laugher.'

HRH The Dalai Lama

Conclusion

Laughter yoga for joy is simple.

It is the simplest form of laughter yoga because there is nothing to learn. You just laugh intentionally and joyfully with increasing awareness. You require no new information and no new knowledge. You already know everything you need. You just need to practise.

This practice is not easy for the same reasons it is so simple. The egoic, monkey mind needs entertainment and distraction, and therefore tends to rebel at this simplicity. It likes to 'learn' in the sense of learning 'things', ie information, knowledge, and exercises. This creates an endless loop where there is always another 'thing' to learn. This can be exhausting and is the opposite of laughter yoga for joy.

Laughter yoga for joy is relaxing. You practise laughing for joy. The archetype of laughter for joy is of course the Laughing Buddha, who just relaxes and laughs joyfully.

It takes practice to relax and so laughter yoga for joy needs sustained practice. Sustained practice needs effort. It takes effort to develop the practice of awareness, also known as mindfulness. It takes further effort to develop the practice of being aware of your awareness, joyfully.

However, after a time effort becomes effortless.

This effortlessness and simplicity are one of the most rewarding practices you can learn. It is learning to learn without 'learning'. It is practising being aware and being guided by your awareness.

It is a profound stillness practice.

In this practice you move, breathe, smile, connect with your awareness and your inner joy, be aware of and be guided by this awareness, connection, and stillness, and express this with a genuine, intentional, joyful laugh.

Please keep practising, joyfully.

'It's okay to wake up laughing'

Anon

'Life is a mirror: if you frown at it, it frowns back; if you smile at it, it returns the greeting'

William Makepeace Thackery

Biography

I am a laughter yoga specialist (Laughter Ambassador and Certified Laughter Yoga Teacher trained by Dr Madan Kataria, Founder of the Global Laughter Yoga movement)

I am the Founder of the Joy Conference (Bristol, UK, 2019).

I am a 2x TEDX Bristol workshop leader.

I am the author of 'Awakening the Laughing Buddha within' and 'Laughter yoga and Happiness: 7 tips from 15 years of laughter yoga'

I am the founder of the Bristol Laughter Club (2003) which is the longest-running series of continuous laughter yoga workshops outside India.

I run regular sessions for organisations and the general public through training courses, conferences, workshops, Retreats and one-to-one sessions.

My own personal wake-up changed my life forever, in one ripping instant. I realised from that spiritual and emotional catharsis that my life was one of service, and all my endeavours have been directed to that end ever since (1991). Even in the most corporate team building and conference environments my agenda has always included encouraging people to connect with their good-natured, creative individuality and perform better not just for themselves but for a bigger picture for the good of all.

Following that thread, my work encourages empowerment, resilience and connection - and joy: helping people see the bigger picture, come alive, be the best they can be, and enjoy the ride. Because this enjoyment is contagious, it gives others permission to enjoy the ride too. It stimulates qualities like connection & kindness, and its ultimate effect is to enhance people's experience of being alive, for the benefit of all.

Over the 40 years of running meetings, delivering conference sessions and providing workshops, my clients have range from the international blue-chip companies (such as Kraft, Bank of Ireland, Novo Nordisk, Lloyds, Continental Airlines), to universities and colleges (including

Bristol, Dundee, U.W.E, Cheltenham Science Festival), to charities and the Healthcare sector (Housing Associations, the NHS, Oxfam, NACTHPC, and others), and to the very experiential end of the spectrum like Glastonbury Festival.

My work regularly appears in the public eye, including

- BBC 2's 'Don't Die Young' with Dr (now Professor) Alice Roberts.
- Radio: BBC Radio 4; BBC Radio2 with Jeremy Vine; Chris Evans; Johnny Walker Show.
- Television: Points West, BBC 1's Inside Out, Discovery Health Channel.
- Printed press: The Sunday Times, The Independent on

Sunday, Nursing Times, Bristol
Evening Post, among others.

In the late 1990's I ran British Medical
Association accredited innovative
('Stress Management with a
Difference') stress management
programmes.

*"Accept responsibility for your life.
Know that it is you who will get you
where you want to go, no one else."*

Les Brown

'I slept and dreamt that life was joy. I awoke and saw that life was service. I acted and behold, service was joy.'

Rabindranath Tagore

Resources

Additional resources are available on www.joehoare.co.uk and www.bristollaughterclub.com

These include:

- The books 'Awakening the Laughing Buddha within' and 'Laughter yoga and happiness: 7 insights from 15 years of laughter yoga'
- YouTube @joehoare27
- Facebook @laughteryogaforjoy
- Instagram: @laughteryogawithjoe
- Linkedin: @laughteryogawithjoe
- Bandcamp vowel meditations, toning and overtone chanting: https://joehoare.bandcamp.co m/follow_me

- Soundcloud - Inner Smile for Relaxation: @joehoare1
- Courses, conferences, Retreats, and coaching
- 'Alchemy of joy' courses
- 'Laughter yoga for joy' masterclasses
- Regular free zoom sessions.

'Sometimes your joy is the source of your smile, but sometimes your smile can be the source of your joy'

Thich Nhat Hanh.

Thank you for reading this book.

I hope you have enjoyed it.

I welcome all comments and feedback, so please feel free to contact me.

Also, please feel free to contact me for the latest updates on coaching, courses, conferences and Masterclasses.

www.joehoare.co.uk

Made in the USA
Las Vegas, NV
03 June 2023

72928473R00046